So, You Want to Write a Book?

A Step-by-Step Method to Life Development

MICHAEL B. GROSSMAN

Nurse Leadership Builders
45 E. City Line Ave.
Bala Cynwyd, PA 19004
www.NurseLeadershipBuilders.com
First Edition

So, You Want to Write a Book?

A Step-by-Step Method to Life Development

Michael B. Grossman
Published by:
Nurse Leadership Builders
45 E. City Line Ave.
Bala Cynwyd, PA 19004
www.Nurseleadershipbuilders.com

GROSSMAN

CONTENTS

GROSSMAN

EXERCISES

GROSSMAN

Dedication

This book is dedicated to Dr. Alan Gruskin, M.D. mentor, colleague, and trusted friend. May his memory and wisdom live on through our deeds, wisdom, and moral obligation to share our words. As Alan said many a time, "You know that's just cute enough a topic to get published!"

GROSSMAN

Forward

If you're ever going to find your greatness, YOU must decide that what you want is bigger AND more important than the fear which prevents you from achieving it.

Gary Ryan Blair
Self-Help Author

As I was writing this book I was again reminded of the beautiful poetry of David Whyte (2012), and my personal journey as an author. I also thought about an exercise in my Kindness book Grossman's (2016): *If you could get anyone to write a forward to your book, from any point in time, who would it be?*
I pondered that question for a few days and decided to use the exercise again. So here it is:

It is a great honor to be asked to write the forward to this latest book by Dr. Grossman. I met Grossman in 1970 when we were just a couple of young college students working at the State Mental Hospital, Byberry. I was in nursing school and Mike was studying psychology. I knew from the start there was something special about him. You know how you meet certain people and have an instant attraction to them? We were like that. We read a lot of the same stuff and were especially intrigued by the dynamics of people, life, work, and trying to figure out the purpose and meaning of life. Mike was taking all these courses in the humanities, philosophy, religion, and psychology. I was focused on the pathophysiology of illness. We had deep conversations and Grossman said he wanted to write books, but was always too busy with his schoolwork. Like an old friend you haven't seen in years our conversations would pick up just like we saw each other yesterday on the unit. I'm not surprised he went on to have an illustrious career, got his doctorate, written a bunch of books, and done research on "difficult" people. He always had an interest in that stuff.

Believe it or not, the last time I saw him was his nursing school graduation in 1975 and the last thing I said to him was "have a good life and make me proud." He lived his part of the bargain and is still living it. I left this world prematurely, unfortunately and hopefully that's a story he'll write about another time.

One of his mentors, Alan Gruskin said, "We have a moral obligation to share our learning's with the world." This book on writing is a long time in the works, but the 40 years of rich experiences are what makes it such a special piece of work. I think it's just the right amount of information to give someone permission and a pathway to writing their first book.

So, congratulations on another job well done. Keep making me proud. Your old buddy...

Lenny Bogle

About the Author

Michael Grossman has been a nursing leader for over 40 years in a variety of clinical settings. Grossman is certified as a Nurse Executive Advance-Board Certified (NEA-BC) and Nurse Manager Leader (CNML). He has worked in a variety of roles including staff nurse, clinical nurse specialist, manager, director, coordinator of leadership development, and nurse entrepreneur. Grossman is a frequent national speaker on a variety of topics including leadership, change, quality improvement, teamwork, and working with emotionally difficult patients and families. Grossman earned his doctoral degree in management of organizational leadership from the University of Phoenix. He is a graduate of Widener University where he received his BSN and MSN in Emergency and Critical Care nursing. He also has a BA from Temple University in Psychology.

Introduction

Life is without meaning. You bring the meaning to it. The meaning of life is whatever you ascribe it to be. Being alive is the meaning.

Joseph Campbell
Comparative Religion Professor

This week I had 3 people ask me how to write a book. They usually ask questions like "should I hire someone to help me get this done?"
"Where do you find a good publisher?"
"What about cover art, do you use a graphic artist?"
"How did you decide on a title?"
"Who did you get to edit your book?"
"What about marketing, I hear publishers do that for you?"
"How did you decide how much to charge for your book?"
        All of these are important questions, but your primary focus should be getting your manuscript written. That is the priority, and the purpose of this book on *how to write a book*. The other questions are just tasks, which can be addressed, easier than you think, once your book is written. For now, they're just distractions that take time away from your writing.

Are You Talking to Me?

        I barely think of myself as an author, so when someone asks me about writing a book, my immediate reaction is *are you talking to me?* Recently I was presenting at a national conference and had a booth in the exhibit hall where I was selling 6 of my books, and 3 course study guides for the course I was teaching at the conference. There were 20 people waiting in line, when someone who had attended my workshop got to the front of the line and said, "Wait, you wrote all of these books?" It was a humbling experience and I felt like a cliché of people I consider *real* authors who say things like "I just sit down, type, and the words just flow." They don't always flow. Some days it's a real chore, some days I'm too exhausted to write, and other times I can go for weeks without writing anything that feels meaningful.

But then there are days like yesterday where I'm talking to a really successful consultant who said she wanted to write a book, didn't know where to begin, and said, "I figured I'd call Dr. Grossman." I asked her if she minded me taking notes while we talked, and I found myself giving the same talk I've given to 100's of different budding authors. As I got to my standard routine around Thomas Huxley's quote, I wondered why I wasn't *doing what I needed to be doing, whether I wanted to or not.* Specifically, I wondered why I hadn't written a book on *How to Write a Book,* so I could just say, "Go on Amazon.com, pick up a copy of my book, and call me back with whatever questions you have."

I thought about that as I drifted off to sleep and listened to a guided meditation from Wayne Dyer where he suggests that *we can manifest what we think about when we go to that place of confidence, quietness, and security that's inside us.* He talked about the *law of attraction* and how *everything we need in life will come to us if we're patient, and believe.* He talked about the things that I discussed in my own books about *confidence, passion, serenity, kindness, gratitude and appreciation.* He suggested that *whatever obstacles appear in life can be overcome.* I woke up this morning thinking about my discussions with Pauline and Lou, about their potential book projects and decided it was time to write my book about *How to Write a Book.*

Much to my surprise, when I opened the My Books folder on my computer, there was already a file on how to write a book and a Word document that was 50 pages long. As I read through that document, I had a hundred thoughts flash through my head of things to include in the book and believe it or not most of them were already in the document. It suddenly struck me that I'd been at this point before. Obviously, I had a discussion with someone last year about how to write a book, took notes, and here they were in my files. So, I spent the last 48 hours (actually 2 weeks) doing a frenzy of writing, while I had the energy and enthusiasm and here it is, done! It may not be perfect, but as they say *the enemy of the good is the perfect* and the only good book is a completed book.

I was thinking about the experience I had in writing *The Emotional Side of Job Loss.* My career coach Rick Hayes suggested I write that book. Rick was a Human Resources professional, a therapist and a minister. Years later I asked him, "Did you suggested I write that as a therapeutic exercise, because it certainly was cathartic?"
He said, "Not really. I just thought you had a lot of insight into the emotional side of job loss and I didn't have a good book on that topic to give my clients!"

How to Use This Book
So, here's my book on *how to write a book.* The rest of the journey is up to you. I'm here to help you on

that journey. I hope my book brings you a lot of *ah ha* insights that you're not alone in this journey and though it may be challenging at times, it can be done and when you are done, there's nothing like the joy of having a discussion with someone about a topic and being able to say, "I wrote a book on that, want a copy?"

I would suggest you read through this book, to get an overview of the process I am suggesting for writing your book. Then, I suggest you go back and re-read the book, this time paying attention to the 15 exercises and actually doing the exercises. While you may be tempted to just get right into writing, the exercises are intended to focus your writing and save you time in the long run.

Thomas Huxley (2001) made a very profound statement about learning life lessons. He said:

> *The most valuable result of all education is to make you do the things you have to do, when it ought to be done, whether you like it or not. It is the first lesson that ought to be learned. And however early a man's (or woman's) training begins, it's probably the last lesson learned thoroughly.*

That's why I am suggesting the most valuable lesson would be to do the 16 exercises, whether you want to or not. My main goal in helping people is to get them on a journey of self-discovery. *You cannot force someone to comprehend a message they're not ready to receive, but you can never underestimate the power of planting a seed.*
Best wishes on your journey…

So, You Want to Write a Book? 19

All of my books are for sale on Amazon.com:

Grossman, M. B. (2017). *Someone's Got to Do the Work Around Here* Bala Cynwyd, PA: Nurse Leadership Builders available at www.amazon.com.

Grossman, M. (2016). *Kindness: Where Has it Gone?* Bala Cynwyd, PA: Nurse Leadership Builders Available at www.amazon.com

Grossman, M. B., & Denno, A. (2013). *I Did All the Work: Why Did They Attack Me?: Scapegoat Theory in the Workplace*. Bala Cynwyd, PA Nurse Leadership Builders available at www.amazon.com.

Grossman, M. B. (2011). *What's Next Create Your Dream Job With a Plan B*. Bala Cynwyd, PA: Nurse Leadership Builders Available on Amazon.com.

Grossman, M. B. (2011). *The Emotional Side of Job Loss*. Bala Cynwyd, PA: Nurse Leadership Builders available at www.amazon.com.

Grossman, M. B. (2011). *Passion: Finding What Energizes Your Career* (1st ed.). Bala Cynwyd, PA: Nurse Leadership Builders available at www.amazon.com.

GROSSMAN

Chapter 1
So, You Want to Write a Book?

Write for yourself, not for a perceived audience. If you do, you'll mostly fall flat on your face, because it's impossible to judge what people want. And you have to read. That's how you learn what is good writing and what is bad. Then the main thing is application. It's hard work.

Wilbur Smith
Historical Fiction Writer

Stephen King said he primarily writes for himself. The fact that people find his writing interesting, and buy his books is a secondary gain. I write, cartoon, and even work in my garden for similar reasons. Having a home vegetable garden is not practical. I can buy tomatoes far cheaper at the store. But, it's about the art of growing my own tomatoes, and picking them when they're green, because I like to pickle tomatoes, and I like my recipe, and I get a feeling of joy when I eat one of my pickled tomatoes. Just like the feeling of joy when someone reads one of my books and comes back and says, "Oh my God that books was exactly what's been troubling me. Thank you."

I often run into people who say, "I've always wanted to write a book, but don't know where to begin. Is that a far-fetched idea?" Not at all. I generally write my books because I run into a number of people asking me the same question, like: *Do you have any tips on changing jobs?* Eventually, I realize there's a need for another book and when the next person who asks me about the same topic, I ask them, "Is it o.k. if I take notes while we talk?" Those notes become the foundation for my next book. In fact, one of the books on my To Write list was: *How to Become a Writer* and I decided to write it after I'd been asked about it yet again.

Julia Cameron asked a great question in her book *The Artist's Way* (2016): At what point do you become a writer, artist, actor, comedian, cartoonist, musician, or whatever your artistic craft is? People often ask me, "Where can I find your cartoons? What newspaper do you work for?" Is that what would make me a *professional* cartoonist? Cameron suggested that the first time someone pays you for your artistic work, you're a "professional." The challenge though, is convincing your *internal saboteur* of that. The *internal saboteur* is that voice of doubt in your head that asks, "Who are you kidding, you're not a writer! Nobody wants to read your drivel. Don't you have better things to do with your time?" I call that voice; *The Evil Witch* and we'll talk more about her later. But, for now you want to write a book, right? Well, I'm here to help.

Narrowing Your Topic

The first step to writing your book is narrowing the focus of the idea for your book. The narrower your focus, the easier it is to write. If your topic is too broad, you won't be able to go into it in depth, and won't really be helping your reader. The more specific your topic, the easier it is to go into it in depth.

Two years ago, I was encouraged to write a book about my leadership philosophies. My immediate thought was about the textbook we used in my doctoral program: Bass's *Handbook of leadership: Theory, research, & managerial applications* (2008). It was a 1,536-page book that covered pretty much anything you could think of related to leadership. But, it was almost too much and the worst part, which we discovered over time, is it really didn't go into any particular topic in depth. So, we ended up using it as a resource tool, and then looking for more specific books and articles on the topics we were learning about in class.

Now I know what you're probably thinking, *but, I have so much to say on my broader topic. If I get too specific, how will I have enough to fill a book?* Before you get too anxious do the next exercise.

EXERCISE #1: *Think of your own experience with reading. Do you tend to read big broad topics, or more specific books? Think of the last topic you wanted to read about…what sort of book did you select?* (Write your answer below).

Suzie and her husband recently moved across the country and she decided to focus on settling into their new home than to look for a job for herself. They have two children ages 3 and 8. She wanted to write a book about her experiences of moving across the country; being a stay at home mom (even though she'd always been a career woman); home schooling; trying to make friends in a new city; and dealing with some of the behavioral issues of her older son. It seemed to me like a lot of different topics to go into a single book and my concern was that if someone was interested in home schooling, for instance, they would want to read more than one chapter about it. Suzie put together 10 topics and started writing her book, but as she talked to people about it, she found they really wanted to know about two specific topics in a lot of detail. They wanted to hear about the emotional journey of staying at home with young kids and they also wanted to know more about Suzie's experience with raising a "spirited" child. Suzie thought there were already more than enough books on "spirited" children, but the more she talked to people about her specific experience, the more she found they appreciated her perspective and that became the focus of her book. The other topics will be in her future books.

Narrowing Your Topic

Figuring out your topic is a process and sometimes it takes an objective outsider to walk you through the process of figuring it out. In the process of writing a book about Interim Leadership, I wrote a chapter on how most leaders are workaholics. It's not the best trait to have, because *good* leaders generally have work-life balance issues. I showed that chapter to a few of my leadership buddies and they all had the same reaction: "This is a chapter? It should be a whole book! It *could* be a whole book." So, I talked to my *muse* and he suggested I take a little detour and see if there was enough in that chapter to produce an entire book. Well, first of all I really didn't know the literature on workaholism, so I did a literature search and quickly discovered that despite all my protesting, I was indeed a workaholic. That's part of the *problem* of workaholism, it's such an acceptable addiction in our society. Who can argue against long hours of work, other than your family who's left behind! So, that chapter turned into my book: **Someone's Got to Do the Work Around Here:** *Overcoming Workaholism.*

Let's do an exercise to narrow your focus:
Exercise #2 Narrowing Your Topic: *Just do a brain dump of all the things you could talk about related to your topic. Let's see how long a list we can create…*(Write your answers below).

GROSSMAN

Chapter 2
Do You Need Permission to Write?

When I am writing best, I really am lost in my world. I lose track of the outside world. I have a difficult time balancing between my real world and the artificial world.

George R. R. Martin
Author Game of Thrones

Good writing is like being in a zone, as George Martin described. It's like having a really, really good conversation that you wish wouldn't end. Julia Cameron began her Artists Way series 25 years ago to help *blocked* artists of any type including writers. She has now written over 40 books! I am indebted to Julia, because her work is what helped me to discover my passion for cartooning and I've brought joy to 1,000's of people through my cartooning work. Cameron's original book focused on *blocked* artists, people who used to paint, draw, or write and had given it up to get down to the *serious business* of life. I have a friend who recently retired and bought a horse farm, and every day she posts pictures on Facebook about her life, her horses, her family, and her gratitude! Cameron's book, *The Right to Write* (1998) is specifically about writer's block. Cameron has also written about the art of leadership and blocked leaders (Bryan, & Cameron, 1998). My own journey with the Artists Way series began in the early 1980's when I attended an all-day workshop by Cameron. I then began the 12-week guided journey of the original Artists Way book. Cameron takes you on a journey of self-discovery through daily journal writing and weekly artist dates. She calls the journal writing *Morning Pages*, because she likes to do them first thing in the morning, to get your day started right. Morning Pages are a form of mindfulness, similar to meditation, yoga, tai chi, or any of the myriad of activities that help you to cultivate focus and get into the flow (Csikszentmihalyi, 2008). Flow is that point where you're in a zone and completely focused on what you are doing. With Morning Pages, the flow happens about 20 minutes into the writing, where you have a burst of energy, and the words just flow onto the paper. What's also magical about the process is insights pop into your head as you are writing, which actually is the point of the process.

My original journey with the Artists Way uncovered my blocked passion for drawing and painting. I did the Artist's Way program in my late 30's because I was intrigued by the thought of what I specifically wanted to do art-wise. I had abandoned my passion for painting, when I got down to the serious business of life, work, and raising a family. Over a 3-month period of journal writing, I discovered what I wanted to do was cartooning. I realized I think in cartoons. I view the world as one giant cartoon drawing and often can't relax until I get that cartoon out of my head and down on paper. Then I feel at peace. Sometimes there's an audience for the cartoon, sometimes it's a small audience of maybe one person who *gets it,* and other times I'm on auto-entertainment; where I'm the only one who sees the humor in it all. The goal of the Artist's Way journey is to find what you are passionate about, and to give yourself permission to do that thing, whatever it may be.

The question you need to ask yourself is are you writing a book for the payoff (to write a bestseller) or are you writing because you enjoy writing? One of the questions I often ask the audience at workshops is: why are there certain things in life we just do, and other things we make so complicated? If you felt like having fried chicken for dinner and there's a great fried chicken place in the neighborhood, would you have to think of the larger implications of having fried chicken? What if you have fried chicken tonight and then a friend asks you out for a fried chicken dinner tomorrow and you've already had chicken? What if they serve chicken at that wedding you're going to on Saturday? You can't have chicken twice in one week, can you? What if the chicken at the wedding isn't as good as the chicken from your local friend chicken place? What if you blurt that out to the family who's hosting the wedding: "Oh My God!!! I just had chicken for dinner!"

The point of my little story is all the *stuff* you're worried about related to writing is just noise, because the most important task you have at the moment is to write. I guarantee you 100% of the books never written, have never been sold! You're not going to get a book contract from a publisher based on a great idea you have with nothing written. They're going to say: "Send me a proposal, or better yet, let me read a few chapters." So, the bottom line is you've got to write the book and stop getting distracted by those nagging questions like: Where will I get it published? Do I need a publisher, an editor, and a printer? Where will I store all the books? How will I ship them? What about marketing, don't I need a publisher to market my book?

How do I know people will like my book? What should I call my book? What will my family think? Do I need a graphic artist to make the cover?

Listen, slow down! All of this is just your internal saboteur trying to undermine you from completing this project. Julia Cameron has an interesting theory about deadlines. She says the beauty of deadlines is they force you to overcome the internal saboteur and tell them: SHUT THE F*CK UP. I HAVE TO GET THIS COMPLETED BY MIDNIGHT! At that point you can just work through all that doubt and appreciate that this is as good as it's going to get and move on.

Exercise #3: *What is the takeaway message from your book? What do you want your readers to remember?* (Write your answer below)

Storytelling

I like to tell stories. They say people remember stories. Psychiatrist Carl Jung said that the brain remembers archetypical stories, which is what dreams are made of. Albert Barnes the great Impressionist art collector had a friend who was his favorite artist. He had him over for dinner once and they sat in Barnes' dining room across from a lovely landscape the artist had painted for him years earlier. The following morning, Barnes woke up and noticed the painting was gone, and asked his friend if he knew where it went. The artist said all through diner he kept looking at that painting and seeing little things he didn't like about it. So, after the household had gone to sleep, he got out his paints and decided to correct the minor flaws. Well, one thing led to another and he'd lost the essence of the painting and decided to just paint over it and start it all over again; a masterpiece lost. The moral of the story is you need to cultivate the ability to be o.k. with your work and to realize you could always do another draft, but at what cost? They say, *the enemy of the good is the perfect.* The point is the difference between draft 9 and draft 27 is probably negligible. We like detail-oriented people in our society, but we also like people who get things done. Remember 100% of perfect books that are never completed, have never been published. That painting Barnes friend made is gone forever, and what a loss that is.

The other interesting story I heard at the Barnes Museum was about Paul Cezanne. They say Cezanne was the ultimate painter; he painted for the sheer joy of painting. He never made a lot of money, he wasn't famous, he just was passionate about painting, and painting in a new style that he invented:

Impressionism. So, where do you begin with your book project?

Sometimes I have trouble getting started on my Morning Pages, so I just start writing about that, *why am I struggling today?* Other mornings I wake up from a vivid dream and wonder, *what was that dream all about?* So, I start my day by writing about that. Sometimes I do Zen Morning Pages, where I just write for an hour and then throw it away. Those writings are sort of like a great conversation with an old friend, where a year later all you remember was you had a great conversation, but the specific content may be lost. I do my writing on my computer, although Cameron originally suggested all writing should be done by hand in a journal. I like having them in my computer, because often times I go back into my Morning Pages file, which is 1,000's of pages at this point, and I can look up something that happened in the past. I'm often surprised by how I remember an event, versus what I wrote at the time, like my brother's death. But actually, that's not so surprising if you read the research by Shermer (2011) on how our brains store information and alter it.

Chapter 3
Why Write?

Writing in a diary is a really strange experience for someone like me. Not only because I've never written anything before, but also because it seems to me that later on neither I nor anyone else will be interested in the musings of a thirteen-year-old schoolgirl.

Ann Frank

Imagine if Ann Frank had never written her diary about her experiences of hiding during the Holocaust? First published in 1947, Frank's journal provided insight into the life of a 13-year hiding in Nazi-occupied Amsterdam. The diary described a little over two years of Ann and her family hiding from the Nazi's in a small space. The appeal of the journal was that it provided insight into the challenges of the war, the Holocaust, and teenage life in general. People connect with her words even today. It reminds me of what author C.S. Lewis once said about writing, "We read to remind us we're not alone" (Attenborough, 1993). Indeed, that is one of the gifts of a good book. It's also something I find with teaching. Every class I teach, there is at least one person who comes up to me afterwards and says, "Thank you for today. I thought I was crazy. You helped me to appreciate that I'm not the only one who thinks this way."

That's why I write, for that one person. I cartoon for that one person too. I can also appreciate your battle with your internal saboteur, because every day I have to remind myself that I'm not trying to save the world, or write a bestseller, or become famous. My gift is to help that one person today.

Exercise #4: *Make a list of 10 people who you think would benefit from reading your book. When you have completed that list make a list of 10 more people who you may not know, who would be likely to want to read your book. What would you like them to take away from the experience of reading your book?*

Are Voices of Doubt a Bad Thing?

We will talk several times in this book about the voices of doubt: *Who cares what I have to say? Do I really have anything unique to say on this topic? Who's going to read my book? I'm not an expert, am I? Is writing really the best use of my time?*

Father Gregory Boyle is a Jesuit Priest who does work in the inner city of L.A. with gang members, most of them with drug and alcohol problems. Father Boyle suggests that we must first "fall down," to provide the opportunity to find our identity and significance in life. He doesn't try to *fix* the inner city, for he believes it provides the opportunity for 30% of his followers to *see the light* in their search for meaning, which is the goal of life. Some believe the second half of life occurs in heaven, but Father Boyle suggests you can live a blessed life here on earth, to prepare you for the next step in heaven. That's what patient's mean when they say, "My nurse is like an angel."

How does that relate to the book you're trying to write? Those voices of doubt may be there to help you narrow your focus. Rather than seeing them as an obstacle, what about seeing them as valid questions to make sure you really are up to this task. I often say this when coaching someone to go after a new job. When the interviewer asks, "Why do you think you're the best candidate for this job," they're not necessarily questioning your ability. They are providing you with the opportunity to convince them of why you are the best candidate. Your book topic is the same way.

My Dissertation Chair said the last step in the process was not "defending" my dissertation. He shared with me that he was convinced I was now the world's leading expert on my particular topic:

Emotionally *Difficult* People. He wasn't asking me to *defend* my views, but to explain them to the Dissertation Committee. It really helped me emotionally to think of them as asking probing questions to understand better, rather than questioning my expertise. That's what I'm hoping you realize in reframing your voices of doubt. Don't let them discourage you from writing. Instead see them as suggestions to provide focus and direction for what to write next.

Chapter 4
The Evil Witch

The Wizard of Oz' is my favorite. It explains what life on this planet is about. Although Dorothy reaches Oz, she finds she had what she needed to go back to Kansas all along, but the Good Witch tells her that she had to learn it for herself. All of the answers to the meaning of life are there.

RuPaul

The theme of the Wizard of Oz, was that the Wizard did not have magical powers, he was just a muse to influence the various characters that they had the ability within themselves to find courage, wisdom, compassion, and a path home.

Arguably the greatest lesson for me from writing morning pages was overcoming the Evil Witch a name I gave to that voice of doubt in my head. I don't even know who she is. I think she's a combination of people, that physically manifests as the person asking me why I bother to write or cartoon. It's that question like, "How much money are you making from that book?" Or, "Can I find your cartoons in the newspaper?" Those sorts of questions trigger the internal saboteur, a term psychiatrist Karl Jung used to describe the voice of doubt in our head. I used my cartooning skills to draw my internal saboteur and remind me not to listen to her!

So, don't be surprised if you start writing your book and your friends and family trigger your own voices of doubt by asking you why you're wasting your time writing a book. What I find ironic is there are so many things in life we could ask the same questions about like: *Why are you watching that T.V. show or reading a book?*

Why did you spend $100 to go to a concert?

Why did you waste your time having that same conversation for the 100ᵗʰ time?

Why does a musician practice their guitar for hours at a time?

Answer: Everything in life isn't about making money! Life is also about being in the moment, talking walks in the woods, looking at flowers, reading poetry, looking at a sunset, watching a baby, relaxing at the beach, going out for a nice dinner with friends, and just spending time with people, just to be with them. Remember the evil witch thrives on you not being effective and wallowing in self-doubt, and pity.

Exercise #5: *How does the Evil Witch manifest for you? What kinds of thoughts enter your head? What methods have you found to combat the Evil Witch?*

Chapter 5
The Emotional Journey

Writing, to me, is like kayaking a river. You are paddling down, and you come to a walled-off canyon, and you make a sharp turn, and you don't know what's around the corner. It could be a waterfall, it could be a big pool. The narrative current carries you. You're surprised, and you're thrilled, and sometimes you're terrified.

Peter Heller
Author

We already talked about writing being an emotional exercise. We will talk later about getting your manuscript published, but I guarantee you nobody has ever published a manuscript they never finished writing. I have a very practical reason why I write. I tend to have a lot of the same conversations over and over again. I often have people stop by my office and ask, "You got a minute?" Then they start a conversation about managing their time, why people are so mean, how to get back the passion in their job, their fear of losing their job, or why they do all the work and then get attacked by their peers. Now that I have 6 books completed on those topics, I talk with them for a bit, and then ask, "Want to read a good book?"

Then, I give them the book I wrote on their topic and ask them to read the book, write down some questions, then come back, and we'll talk again. 80% of them never come back, they just want to stop by periodically to reduce their anxiety with a nice chat, but they really don't want to do anything about their problem. But there's that 20% who come back and say, "I loved your book. I did all the exercises, and just have few questions." That's the kick for me. Those are the people who go back to school, change jobs, rekindle the passion in their work, and yes write books!

Channeling Your Emotion

There is a lot of emotion involved in writing, most of it is that inner voice that questions whether your writing is relevant and whether anyone will read it. Let's not make this more complicated than it has to be. Why do we make writing so complicated? Do you have to think before you speak? While, some people are shy and do fret over what to say, in general most adults learn how to have conversations where the words just flow. Hopefully you are writing your book on a topic you are familiar with and confident to speak about. The goal is finding a method in which it is easy for you to get your thoughts from your head down onto paper. Some people like writing long hand on a notebook, others like using a computer. I have a friend who's a school psychologist and doesn't mind if her high school students communicate via text messaging, the telephone, or even through drawings. Whatever they feel comfortable doing, to communicate is acceptable to her. The key is to write. Some tips to get you started are:

1. Send yourself a message. You can type it out or use the dictation feature on your smart phone. You can access it a few different ways:
   a. Record a voice message
   b. Type yourself a text message

      c. Send yourself a text message using the dictate feature in text messaging

      d. Send yourself an email via your phone. Most email systems also have a dictation feature

2. Talk to someone about your topic. Just have a conversation about your topic, and take notes, or have them take the notes for you, then read it back to you: "You said…"

3. Journaling is a great way to do your writing. First of all, journaling is a good way to practice writing and to feel more comfortable putting your thoughts into words. Ideally a journal is a personal relationship between you and your journal, which helps to overcome some of the anxiety around what other people think of your writing.

4. One of my favorite exercises is something I use to overcome writer's block. I just start writing in my journal about why I can't seem to write today. Usually, within 20 minutes I find myself writing again and get back on track.

Don't assume you are going to produce a finished copy in the first sitting. It usually takes 7-9 drafts to get to a good product. Abraham Lincoln said it takes 2 weeks to write a good impromptu speech. That sounds about right to me.

Overcoming Shyness

I was shy growing up and met my really outgoing friend Lenny Bogle when I was in my early 20's. Lenny taught me a technique to overcome my shyness that I use to overcome writer's block. He said to think about your audience. "Who's likely to be at tonight's party? What kind of work do they do? What sorts of hobbies and interest do they have? He'd have me write this all out on a 3x5 card, in a tiny notebook, or on a napkin. Today, I put most of those ideas in notes on my smartphone. The other key to that approach was Lenny read a lot on different topics. He read several magazines a week like Newsweek, Time, Scientific American, Psychology Today, and Popular Mechanics. Those magazines gave him an overview of a variety of topics, which made it easy to say, "I just read an article on that." Today this is so much easier with the Internet, where you can easily keep up to date on a variety of topics. The importance of all this to writing is you have a built-in conversation starter of saying to someone, "I'm actually writing a book on _____," and then seeing if they have some ideas they can contribute to your book or suggestions for topics to include in it. On the next page is an exercise to help you identify some challenges and solutions.

Exercise #6: *What sorts of emotional challenges do you have with life in general? What have you found is effective to overcome them? Have you found anyone who can help you with your emotional struggles? Do you know any writers who can support you?*

Chapter 6
I Have So Many Ideas
Where Do I Start?

Most of the important things in the world have been accomplished by people who have kept on trying when there seemed to be no hope at all. Inaction breeds doubt and fear. Action breeds confidence and courage. If you want to conquer fear, do not sit home and think about it. Go out and get busy.

Dale Carnegie
Author: How to Win Friends and Influence People

Just start; that's how you start. Look at this piece I wrote on a day when I felt blocked:

I sat in front of my computer for what seemed like an eternity. I just couldn't seem to get the words to come. My brain was like a complete blank. I felt like I had this story inside me, but couldn't get it started. All I could think about was yesterday going to see my brother in the hospital and seeing him lying there in bed, so helpless, so tired, it just wasn't the vital, vibrant brother I'd grown up with. What happened. How did he get this sick, why him, why now in the prime of his life? I couldn't get it out of my head, that imagine of him and yet I had a task to do. I had to get this chapter written for a textbook. It was such an honor for them to ask me to write it. How was I going to explain to them I was paralyzed and just couldn't write?

Early in my leadership career I took the Dale Carnegie course based on his famous book: *How to Win Friends and Influence People* (1998). Carnegie wrote that book in 1936 and is famous for quotes like:

Success is getting what you want. Happiness is wanting what you get.

Remember, today is the tomorrow you worried about yesterday.

If you want to conquer fear, don't sit home and think about it. Go out and get busy.

People rarely succeed unless they have fun in what they are doing.

Any fool can criticize, condemn, and complain but it takes character and self-control to be understanding and forgiving.

You can make more friends in two months by becoming interested in other people than you can in two years by trying to get other people interested in you.

Develop success from failures. Discouragement and failure are two of the surest stepping stones to success.

In the Dale Carnegie course, we had to do two talks a week, because they recognized the importance of public speaking. In class they taught us to get right into the story. They said not to spend a lot of time on background. If a story needs a lot of background, it's not a good story. Think about a good action thriller, be it a book or movie. They get you right into the action. I personally don't like a book that takes 150 pages of background before they get into the story. So, what gets in the way of telling our story?

Ram Dass (1988) suggested your guru appears in many disguises. One of those disguises is the Evil Witch. The evil witch manifests in some rather subtle and creative ways including overwhelming you with too choices of where to begin. There's an old Native

American tale about the best way to cross a rapidly flowing stream: *Just cross!* So, I say, *Just Write!!!*

It's easy to get stuck sitting in front of your computer ruminating about that opening line. There's a simple solution. JUST WRITE and worry about the grammar and details later. Ruminating is just an annoying way of avoiding doing the *real* work.

But What Should I Write About?

Pat Williams was the General Manager of the Philadelphia 76ers basketball team that won the world championship in 1983. Since that time, he has written 100 books on leadership and motivation. I heard him asked at one point how he does it? He said he has a master list of all his book ideas and when he gets a new idea, he just adds it the list and goes back to working on his current project. I adopted a similar approach a few years ago. I have a file in my computer called *My Books* and in there is a separate sub-file for each book title. Some days, like today my journal entry was devoted to writing about a book about writing a book. So, that's what I worked on.

I thought about the last conversation I had with a successful consultant about her writing a book.

I asked her, "How long was your doctoral dissertation?" She said 250 pages!

I said, "So clearly, you know how to write! It's the rest of the *stuff* that's getting in the way.

Sometimes, I will cut and paste from my journal writings into a specific book file. Other times I read a good article on the specific topic, so I put that into my books to write files. I try to remain focused on the current book I am writing, but I'll be honest, sometimes I take a little detour and start working on a future book, because I have an idea in my head and want to get it down on paper, before I forget it or lose the emotion in it.

Exercise #7: *What gets in the way of you telling your story?*

Forced Choice Inventory

Forced choice inventory is a technique that is used when trying to choose between items of apparently equal value or importance. Some examples I often encounter are people trying to decide which factors are most important in a career choice; what major to select in graduate school, what is the most important skill to focus on first in a leadership-training program, or what topic to choose to write about. Personally, I think you should assume you're going to write multiple books, so it's less important which one you write first. The forced choice approach is used when stakes are at either end of being a very important choice, or of little consequence and you are having difficulty making choices. Either all the choices are important or there is little significance to choosing one over the other. The forced choice inventory requires that you match options and make a choice. One common use of forced choice inventory is after a brainstorming session in which there is a long list of high priority items. Forced choice can be used to decide which item is the most important to address first.

Choosing a Topic for Your Book

Chris had thought about writing a book for about 10 years. She had so many potential topics, all of which she felt were important. I reminded Chris that we went through a similar process when she was trying to decide on graduate school. She wasn't sure if she wanted to be a Nurse Practitioner, a Clinical Specialist, an educator, or go into management.
"I like all of them," Chris said.
"I think about being an educator, but then I think it's too narrow because I also like patient care, which is

why I think maybe I should be a nurse practitioner, but that's not quite it either because I don't want to leave the bedside, which is why I think a Clinical Specialist might be the ideal role, but then I worry about whether there will be enough job opportunities? I also think I should just go back to school for my MBA and do management. There's always good jobs in management."

Chris's dilemma is not uncommon, especially when you throw social desirability into the equation. Social desirability is the phenomenon of subjects making a choice based on what they perceive as the accepted choice by their peers and society. Therefore, in this example Chris may choose to become a nurse practitioner because that is the perceived *right* career choice on her particular unit. Chris commented, "Well everybody else is going to grad school to become a nurse practitioner, so I guess that's what I should just do." The question was what did Chris really want to do?

Working with Chris, we constructed a forced choice inventory grid based on the components of each career choice. For the purposes of this example the list was reduced to only five items, however my experience is that this works best with 8-10 items. Chris had narrowed her choices to Nurse Practitioner or Nurse Educator:

	Patients	Develop Staff	Physiology	Learning Theory	Clinic
Patients					
Develop Staff					
Physiology					
Learning Theory					
Clinic					

We then asked Chris to force a choice between two option such as "Would you rather take a course on Developing Staff or Physiology of Diseases?"
Chris said, "I like both!"
Coach: "That's the point, you have to make a choice of one over the other, a forced choice."
Here is Chris's completed chart:

	Patients	Develop Staff	Physiology	Learning Theory	Clinic	RESULT
Patients					X	1
Develop Staff	X		X	X	X	4
Physiology	X				X	2
Learning Theory	X		X		X	3
Clinic						0

Chris rated each item against the other 4 and base on this information, it looked like Chris preferred the courses related to education and we encouraged her to get an education degree.

So Many Topics

Let us join Chris a few years later as she discusses topics for her first book:
Coach: *So, Chris we made a list of key topics you've come up with from our brainstorming session. There's a lot of overlap in the book topics and certainly you could write one book covering all these topics, but it would be better to narrow your focus.*
Rather than focus on the book right now, we asked Chris which topic she was more passionate talking about? Let's say she was meeting with a group of new nurses, what topic would she want to talk about? By

forcing Chris to choose between one topic or the other the results looked like this:

	Helping New Graduates	Mentoring	Graduate School Choices	Changing Jobs	Bullying	RESULTS
Helping New Graduates			X	X		2
Mentoring	X		X	X		3
Graduate School Choices						0
Changing Jobs			X			1
Bullying	X	X	X	X	X	5

Chris: *See that is the problem. I like talking about all of these topics. There's not one thing I really want to talk about more than the others.*

Coach: *O.K. I understand that, but for this exercise, I want you to force yourself to choose one over the other. So, let me paint the scenario: It's Monday morning, there is a new set of orientees, it is also really busy on the unit, and a patient with one of your favorite diagnoses was admitted. Your manager asks you what you want to do today. Would you rather work on designing a workshop on mentoring, a general workshop on helping new nurses, or something on bullying?*

Chris: *Well I like developing young nurses AND I like the mentoring, but if I had to choose, I think I would work on the specifics of bullying, because I think people really don't understand the dynamics. However, I am not sure if that is the right choice?*

Coach: *Just hang in there. Let us do a few more and this will start to make more sense. So, would you rather talk to them about changing jobs or the perils of bullying?*

Chris: *Well I think choosing the right job is important, but if you don't stand up to bullies, your career can't go anywhere. Yes, I think Bullying is the priority. I love the look on their faces when I explain a concept like bullying that they learned about in school, can match it up to what is happening today on their unit, and can see where my practical solutions can help them right now.*

Coach: *O.K. great, let's keep going. What about bullying vs graduate school choices?*

Chris: *Well see here is the dilemma again. I would love to talk to them about graduate school, but if a bully destroys them in their first year, they're never lasting long enough to think about graduate school.*

Coach: *O.K. I have two comments. Number one, try to avoid making this an either or. We're not saying you're never going to write about the other topics, it's just not your first priority. Maybe there is a way you can do both, like the book is primarily about bullying and you'll also talk about mentoring and how a mentor can help you with bullies. But the primary focus is on bullying.*

Chris: *I think I would like to do more research on the bullying literature.*

Coach: *GREAT! That's what I like to hear. O.K. the last one would you rather write about bullying or mentoring?*

Chris: *Hmmmm, that's a tough one, because mentors are really important. But, I think the deciding factor is what I'm the most passionate about right now. Right now, I'd rather do some more research on bullying and then, I'll look into mentoring some more.*

Chris's choice about what to write about is just one example of using forced choice inventory methodology. It is a simple technique that can be done quickly on a piece of paper by drawing your own grids and adding labels. What is important is to focus on where the person derives their energy and passion. You can use this technique for a variety of things where you're not sure what choice you want to make. It eliminates the unnecessary ruminating about making a choice, and gets you into the action phase of writing, which is where we want to be. You want to choose the one that is going to excite you the most. It is easier to complete things when you are passionate about them versus doing it because it is what everybody else thinks you should do. That is the essence of what the forced choice inventory pushes you to do.

Exercise #8: Fill out a Forced Choice Inventory on your issues.

	XXXXX	XXXXX	XXXXX	XXXXX	XXXXX	RESULTS
XXXXX						
XXXXX						
XXXXX						
XXXXX						
XXXXX						

Chapter 7
Are You Really an Author?

I looked at myself, and I just said, 'Well, you know, I can sing, but I'm not the greatest singer in the world. I can play guitar very well, but I'm not the greatest guitar player in the world.' So, I said, 'Well, if I'm going to project an individuality, it's going to have to be in my writing.'

Bruce Springsteen

Bruce Springsteen is a great example of someone questioning their artistic ability. Imposter Syndrome was first described in the late 1800's as a psychological set of behaviors where an individual doubts the validity of their accomplishments and fears being exposed as a fraud, or imposter. Despite all the evidence of their success, they still rationalize it is luck, deception, or people thinking they're smarter than they actually are. Imposter syndrome is complicated by negative feedback from people who are jealous, resentful, and vindictive. But, much of the phenomenon is internal, in the victim's thoughts.

This is another way the evil witch manifests. Someone hears you're writing a new book and starts interrogating you about the logistics of it all: How much does your book sell for? How much profit do you make? Is it enough to retire on? Are you on the New York Times Bestseller List? Do you have any book signings coming up? Are you on tour? Have any famous authors contacted you? Who would you say your writing is most like?

Julia Cameron addressed this in her Artist Way series. She suggested you go back and look at some

famous peoples first works. For instance, she says to get a copy of George Lucas's graduate school film project. That's where he started his Star Wars career. So, was he a "professional" movie maker at that point? What makes you a "professional" author? Is it the first time someone pays you $20 for a book? The same goes for an artist, doesn't it? The first painting you sell defines you as an artist. But, I think it's the wrong line of questions. Here are the questions I like to ask someone as they're writing their first book:
Isn't it great to see your thoughts down on paper?
Have you had some brilliant insights as you've been writing, things you hadn't anticipated till you started writing?
Can you picture the completed book?
Have you made a draft of your book cover?
Have you given what you've written so far to some of your fans, who you know will provide you with encouragement?

This is a very important point, you need to be very careful who you talk to because we often have people in our lives who discourage us. My mother told me once, "I want to give you some feedback. I gave your book to a friend of mine and she loved it. But, then she started asking me some specific questions and I didn't know what to say, because I really never read your book. I just glanced at it and gave it to Shirley." Oh my God! How devastating do you think it was to hear that from my own mother?
Ugh! But, it was a valuable lesson. I don't use her as a barometer. I know she's really proud of me because she brags about me to other people, but I really don't care to sit her on the virtual psychiatrist couch and discussion my relationship with my mother. That's further down the book project list. Although, I did write a book with my mother that has her favorite 100

stories that she repeats over and over and over again (Grossman, 2011).

Exercise #9: What are some ways in which you doubt your own authenticity to be a writer? Give 10 examples of things you've done you didn't think you could accomplish. Who are some people who unconditionally support you and will be a support for your writing project? (Provide your answer below).

Chapter 8
Where Do I Begin?

I have a problem with beginnings... and endings... and middles. But I don't know what else I would do. I find it very, very difficult to write. It takes everything; it's physically and mentally and emotionally exhausting for me. And my neighbors. And my dog.

Miriam Toews
Fiction Writer

Indeed, writing is challenging. But, it doesn't have to become a chore. If it becomes too much like *work,* it's not fun anymore and to me, that's a good point to take a step back and ask yourself if you're writing on the right topic. Writing should be a labor of love. It should feel inspiring to have your words appear on paper. Now don't get me wrong, it doesn't always feel that way and sometimes there are portions of a book that are challenging, because it brings up old wounds and things you don't really want to talk about. But, still in the end, hopefully you take a step back and say, "I'm glad I got that off my chest!"

The beginning is often a challenge, because it's just too wide open. You can write about anything, there's just too many choices. It's like standing in the spaghetti sauces section of the supermarket...just too many choices. I like to break that ruminating cycle by doing a mindmap and getting all the choices down on paper. Mindmapping is a form of brainstorming, that is a bit more creative than a typical to do list. Here's an example:

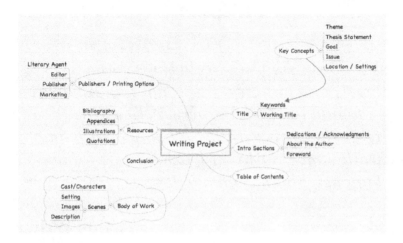

Mindmapping mimics the way a typical mind works. Think about as you're falling off to sleep or trying to meditate and 100's of thoughts pass through your mind, like clouds in the sky. Most people don't think in a sequence, like a typical To Do list. Mindmaps provide a visual representation of the various categories and allow you to jump around as the thoughts enter your head. The other beauty of Mindmapping is it enhances the process of brainstorming, which is making a list of ideas, without judgment or feedback. Brainstorming is just a dumping of ideas in rapid succession.

Exercise #10: *Make a Mindmap of ideas for your book. Just start the way we did in our example above, with a heading like Writing Project and then branch off into the various subcategories. Don't be afraid to spend a bit of time on this project. You can get back to writing your book once you have this exercise completed.*

Getting Down to Business

I have a template for my typical 150-page book. I like to write what my colleague Louise Jakubik calls *Airplane* Books. They're books that you can read on a cross country plane trip. I also like to sell my books for $19.95, because then I can just sell someone a copy on the spot for $20, at a workshop for instance or right out of my backpack. Now that I have 6 books completed, I have a Word file that is a template for future projects including:

- Cover Page
- Table of Contents
- Dedication
- Forward
- About the Author
- Introduction
- Chapters (I usually do about 10)
- References.

If you want that format, let me know and I'll give you my template. But you can also find a blank template on most of the self-publishing websites.

The important point here is the Evil Witch wants you to get bogged down in the details rather than focusing on the writing. Remember, the Evil Witch thrives on you not changing, but remaining the same. So, every time you get bogged down in the details and paralyzed to write, the Evil Witch has won!

Chapter 9
Developing a System

Writing is work. It takes a lot of contemplation, concentration, and out-and-out sweat. People tend to romanticize it, that somehow your work appears by benefit of some mystical external force. In reality, to be a writer, you have to sit down and write. It's work, and often it's hard work.

Wendelin Van Draanen
Award-Winning Children's Author

Every writer has a system for how they get their work done. You have to come up with yours. I've been doing Morning Pages for 25 years now, and like meditation, I can do it pretty much anywhere. But, to get started with your writing, you probably need a time and a place where you can write, uninterrupted for at least an hour at a time. I am an early morning person, so I get up at 4 a.m. and get right into my writing. I can often get a few hours of writing done before my family wakes up. But, I know some night owls who do their best writing after midnight.

Graham Greene the famous 20th-century British writer always wrote 500 words a day then stopped. He said the mechanics of that was a tool to avoid spending 15 hours ruminating about one sentence and worrying about how it sounded. If you think about it 500 words a day would add up to over 182,000 words in a year which would be close to 400 pages! Greene wrote 25 novels over his 67-year writing career.

I do dissertation work with people struggling to complete their dissertation. It is much like working with people struggling with a diet and exercise routine. You can't get hung up if you fall off your diet for a day. You need to just get back to it. Page-a-day writing is the same phenomenon. The key is keeping your momentum because if you fall behind for a few days or weeks it takes too much inertia to review where you were at and start up again. My point is I am in support as a writer, with total emersion, but with the qualification that it also includes appropriate break times.

The Impact of Fatigue

It's very hard to write when you are overwhelmed and stressed. It's why schools originally gave teachers the summer off to recharge their batteries, so to speak. Unfortunately, many teachers work a second job in the summer. Another solution in academia is the sabbatical, which was also designed to provide a time away from all the stresses of work and life, to devote time to learning and writing. I am a workaholic. I'm in workaholism recovery, but it's a long process (Grossman, 2017). So, there are long periods of time where I am too exhausted to do something creative like writing. It has been suggested it's about managing your energy, not your time, which we will discuss in the next chapter.

The Przybelinski Method

Dr. Steve Przybelinski is an Aeronautical Engineer and university professor who has an interesting approach to academic writing. I pretty much follow his method for writing each of my paragraphs. He suggests each paragraph should look something like this:

1. The first sentence is a reference to the literature with a quote or an *objective fact*
2. The second sentence is an *observation* about the objective fact
3. The third sentence is an *interpretation*, in your own words
4. The fourth sentence is an *observation* of your interpretation
5. The fifth sentence summarizes the point of the paragraph. It should contain the takeaway message for your reader.
6. The sixth sentence is a connector to the next paragraph, where you will repeat the same process.

Przybelinski was a classmate in my doctoral program and had an interesting perspective on the daunting task or writing our dissertations. He said, "At this point, you can write a 20-page paper easily, right?" Of course, I could after 3 years of doctoral classes. He went on to say, "Well your introduction is like one 20-page paper. Then your literature review is like two 20-page papers. The methodology section is a 20-page paper, the results is two 20-page papers, and the summary is another 20-page paper. When you break it down like that, the daunting task seems manageable. It's like the old joke about *how do you eat an elephant?*

Answer: *One bite at a time.*
That's how you write a book. You break it down into
tiny pieces, rather than focus on the daunting task.

What About Fiction Writing?

There is a certain amount of overlap between
fiction and nonfiction. Part of that reason is that no
writing is truly objective, it's always someone's
interpretation of the information and what happened
historically. I often think what it would be like if a
reporter followed me around, interviewed people, and
then wrote their interpretation of what happened.
Shermer (2011) wrote a brilliant research book about
the believing brain, in which he presented extensive
neurological research on how people remember things
in a different way than they actually may have
occurred. It's one of the challenges of writing about
things that happened in the past.

I went to a workshop with one of my favorite
fiction authors Nelson DeMille. My favorite DeMille
books was a Word of Honor (1998), a fictional story of a
Vietnam veteran who wrote a bestseller that included
the story of a massacre. It was supposed to be fiction,
however some of his fellow soldiers came forward and
said the story her referred to was pretty close to what
actually happened in Vietnam. DeMille said it was
pretty close to his process for writing fiction. He said
that a lot of his work is based on things that actually
happened, but he'd rather not get into a debate about
the accuracy of his work, so he changes the names,
some of the details, and adds a qualifier at the
beginning of the book that it's fiction and any relation
to real people is merely coincidental. It gets back to a
question we asked earlier in Exercise #3 which was

what is the takeaway message from your book? What's the one thing you want the reader to remember from reading your book. Sometimes, fiction does a better job of presenting a theme and getting across a message by removing the debate as to whether the history is accurate or not. If you think about some of the recent books that have been written by controversial political figures, so much of the debate is about whether the books are accurate or not, rather than focusing on their key message.

Tips for Writing Fiction

Much of the attraction of a good novel is the way in which the writer uses words to spark your imagination and paint a picture in your head of what is going on. There are a few tips for doing that. One of them is to write about something you know about, such as your hometown, where are you currently live, or someplace you've traveled to. Rather than just saying: "We were at the park," describe the park, what it looked like, how it smelled like, and any outstanding features, and who else was there.

Characters are a central part of a good novel and the more people can relate to the characters the more they are captivated by the story. That doesn't mean they have to like the character. They can just be interested in the character's story and try to understand how something like the story could happen. A good way to do this is to loosely base your characters on people you know or have experienced. Start by writing a paragraph or two describing your key characters. One way to do that is to mix and match your characters based on people you know or have known in the past. So perhaps you're writing about your friend Joe, but you change his name in your novel to Mary, and change his gender to be a woman. This takes some creativity because now you have to alter Joe's behavior slightly so that he is more feminine. You can base his behaviors on a female in your current or past history. Now to further complicate this, or make it interesting you can embellish your character's behavior to address your theme based upon something that happened in your past but embellishing the story to make it interesting to the reader. Some people find writing fiction overcomes some of their anxiety and pressure from their internal critic. The approach, in general is still the same. You want to identify your topic, your key message, outline your chapters, and remain open to the possibility of changing direction as you write. Being comfortable with the magical surprises that appear as you write is a skill that comes with time.

Exercise 11: Let's do some brainstorming around your characters.
Character #1:
- What is there name?
- Whose personality are they based on? You can choose multiple personalities of people you know.
- What do they look like, again you can choose to make them a composite of several people you know.
- What setting are you in? Is it a real city or town, or a fictional location based on several places you've been?
- Be as detailed as possible, as it brings life to your writing.

Chapter 10
Manage Your Energy
Not Your Time

When people start writing there is this idea that you have to get everything right first time, every sentence has to be perfect, every paragraph has to be perfect, every chapter has to be perfect, but what you're doing is not any kind of public show, until you're ready for it.

Irvine Welsh
Scottish Novelist

Ned Bachus (2017) was a writing professor for 40 years and said the #1 thing he taught his students was that writing takes more than one draft. He would give his students feedback on their work, then say if you want to know your grade you need to come see me in my office. When they came to his office, he would ask them how they went about writing their paper. Then he would share with them how the best writers in class approached their writing project, through multiple drafts. Of course, that means you can't wait till the last minute to do your writing. I think of writing like reading a good novel or watching a good television series. When I get to the end of a good novel, I wish it wasn't ending. I feel the same way about a good writing project. I so enjoy the journey, I'm not eager for it to end. Although, I don't want the project to go on forever, because the only good book project is a completed one. One of the reasons I want to complete my book project is I have other book projects lined up to do.

Managing Your Energy

Jim Loehr was the psychologist for the U.S. Olympic Team. He looked at how athletes prepare for long distance events, like running marathons, by practicing in short sprints. He suggested the key to getting things done is working in short intervals (90 minutes), with 30-minute breaks to reenergize yourself. It's all about managing your energy to be at your peak, not working straight through (Loehr & Schwartz, 2004). I had a professor who suggested writing our doctoral dissertations in a page a day. He suggested writing one page, every day. Some days you might write 10 pages. But you needed to do at least one page a day. If you had a long day and started to fall asleep and realized you had not written your page, he suggested you get up and write a page. His point was to keep your momentum going, because once you lose your momentum on a massive project it's hard to get it going again. That's why I like to make a draft outline of my chapters, so I can work on a chapter as the mode hits me. I don't always work on my chapters in order, I tend to work on them more in terms of my mood. So, for instance let's say I had a bad day at work and am feeling sad or depressed. That's a good opportunity to write that chapter about that sort of mood, as opposed to trying to write about being positive and passionate.

Exercise 12: *Let's map out a typical day using the Jim Loehr method of working in 90-minute intervals with strategic breaks. Let's assume for the purposes of this exercise that you have an entire day free:*

8:00 Writing
9:30 Break (what activity will you do?)
10:00 Writing
10:30 Break (what activity will you do?)
11:00 Writing
11:30 Break (what activity will you do?)
12:00 Writing
1:30 Break (what activity will you do?)
2:00 Writing
3:30 Break (what activity will you do?)
4:00 Writing
5:30 Break (what activity will you do?)
7:00 Writing
8:30 Break (what activity will you do?)
9:00 Writing
10:30 Break (what activity will you do?)

You can break down this exercise into smaller intervals, such as just writing in the morning, or evening depending on your work schedule.

Kristin started graduate school and quit after a couple of semesters, because she said it was interfering too much, with her family life. She had young children and was driven to have school be perfect and felt guilty, that translated into general crankiness, which her husband resented. He was very supportive because she had been supportive of him while he attended the Police Academy 2 years prior. She was doing schoolwork on the weekends, leaving dinner early, asking him to clean up the kitchen, and put the kids to sleep. She realized it wasn't fair, not at this stage while her kids were so young. So, she stopped school. A few months later I was teaching a class and Kristin mentioned something she'd experience in graduate school. I said, "Wait, your back in school?"

She said she realized she needed to manage her time differently, so it didn't impact so much on her family life. So, she said she started doing school work early in the morning, before her family woke up. She also worked for an hour late at night, after the kids and her husband went to sleep. She also put her work on a portable hard drive, and did work during her lunch break. She stayed at work for an extra hour some days, and did her schoolwork in an empty office to avoid going home and getting caught up in home activities. Ironically, after she found better balance in her life, her grades were even higher, because she was more relaxed once she removed the self-pressure.

While Kristin's story was about schoolwork, the same principles apply to writing a book. You need to find devoted time for your writing, that doesn't interfere with the other parts of your life.

Chapter 11
What About a Publisher?

I'm looking for backing for an unauthorized auto-biography that I am writing. Hopefully, this will sell in such huge numbers that I will be able to sue myself for an extraordinary amount of money and finance the film version in which I will play everybody.

David Bowie
Musician

David Bowie was an innovative musician who broke many of the conventional rules of his time. Sometimes I wonder how Bowie overcame listening to the so-called experts of his time about how to write music and just did his own thing?

Years ago, I was on a plane and about two hours into the flight the guy next to me asked, "What are you writing? Looks like a book?"

"Indeed, it is," I replied. "It's a book about the emotional side of job loss."

He asked me why I was writing on that topic, what I did for a living, and if I had a network of potential buyers for the finished product. He said, "I hope you're self-publishing it."

I asked him what he did for a living and he said he was a publisher. I was pretty surprised he was suggesting I self-publish.

He then told me he published a book a few years ago on communication skills for clinicians, written by a nurse. He thought it was a really good book, but it didn't sell. He said he had 10,000 copies in a warehouse and couldn't even sell them to discount books stores. He suggested if you're selling a technical book and you are a member of the community, like nursing, who would buy the book, by all means just publish it yourself.

Self-Publishing Companies

About 10 years ago a new printing machine was invented that printed books on demand. It's like a copy machine, that prints books. CreateSpace, the company that did the publishing in the U.S., eventually was purchased by Amazon.com. It's now called KindleDirect Publishing. I happen to use them, but there are other similar companies out there. It revolutionized publishing. No longer do writers need to find a publisher, or pay thousands of dollars to print their book, and pay for warehouse space to store their books. Do you know how much the writer actually gets at the end of the stream of traditional publishing? I have two friends who published award-winning textbooks in the traditional way, through publishers and make about $2 for every book they sell, despite the fact the books sell for $50.

With CreateSpace you send them your completed manuscript online, figure out the pricing and distribution path, and they print copies as the orders come in. There is nothing printed in advance. If you list your book on Amazon.com it can be delivered to the customer the following day or can be delivered instantly if your book is converted to the Kindle edition. There is no outlay of money! Of course, CreateSpace takes their fee, but it is far less than the cut a traditional publisher takes. I'm sure you're thinking, *but the publisher markets and distributes your book?* Not necessarily, they only aggressively market their top sellers. The remainder are like the guy I met on the plane, who expects the writer, to drum up interest. You don't need to buy books in advance, don't need a warehouse, and if you find a mistake in your book you can just correct it and all the books moving forward will have the correction. It has really shifted the paradigms around publishing.

Distribution

I sell my books on Amazon.com. I don't make as much money, but I'm not trying to make a living as a writer, and I'm willing to sacrifice profits to not be my own book distribution center. When someone asks me where they can find my books, I send them to amazon.com and they do the rest. There's even a program for converting your book to a Kindle version, because today more and more folks are reading books on their electronic devices. Indeed, the world of publishing has changed.

Chapter 12
Gratitude

*And the idea of just wandering off to a cafe
with a notebook and writing and seeing where
that takes me for a while is just bliss.*

J. K. Rowling

A.J. Jacobs (2018) is a senior writer at Esquire
Magazine and has written several New York Times
bestsellers. Arguably his greatest work was about
gratitude and the fact that we don't take enough time
out of our lives to express our gratitude. Jacobs decided
to trace the path of his morning cup of coffee and to
express his gratitude to the 1,000 people who were
responsible for his morning cup of coffee. Jacobs
suggested if we're going to focus on the negatives in
life, then we need to pay equal attention to the positive
things also. He studied the history of coffee and how it
was prepared 100 years ago. He went to the coffee
warehouse and thanked the night shift janitor for
keeping the place clean, so his coffee didn't have rat
droppings in it. He thanked the farmers, the coffee
pickers, the coffee roaster, the distributor, the truck
driver, basically everyone who is some way was
involved in his cup of coffee. It was a mind-boggling
experience. But the other thing I learned from A.J.
Jacobs, which I heard in a podcast he did, was his
thoughts on publishing. He said he appreciates
everyone who played a part in publishing his books,
but he was tired of people telling him their formula for
success. He was tired of being told how to write, what
to say, how to say it, and what were the keys to success.
The problem was the so-called experts, were experts on

what worked in the past, which is not necessarily what is going to make for a bestseller in the future.

He also had reached a point where it wasn't about the money. He wanted to publish his story, in the way he wanted to publish it, which is why he now self-publishes. Now, you could say, "Well that's easy for him to say, he's a bestseller." Don't get me wrong, I'm not suggesting you should ignore input, as all feedback is valuable and something to express your gratitude for. But, J.K. Rowling's was told by 100's of publishers that you can't write kid's books about witchcraft and sorcery. Cezanne was told that impressionist painting was not realistic enough. The Kentucky Colonel's fried chicken recipe was rejected 100's of times by food manufacturers and restaurateurs. The list goes on and on, and my point is this: If you have an idea for a book, just write it and self-publish it, and if it's really good, you can take it to a publisher later.

It is not for us to understand the nature of the universe, but just to accept it. That's often easier said than done. My daughter just went to a mindfulness workshop and said, "Dad you really don't have to DO anything about anything, whatever it is that's going on. You can just be mindful, patient, and allow life to unfold." Indeed, that is true. A.J. Jacobs suggested it's a good idea to express your gratitude both to people face-to-face and in your writing. As C.S. Lewis said, "We read to remind us we're not alone." I have a lot of gratitude for the good things in my life that manifest every day. It's hard at times to remind myself of that. I think of the women who said, "I always think about what you said in your book?"
"What's that," I asked.

She said that she was struggling with her job and asked me what I wanted her to do and I said, "It's not about what I want you to do, it's about what you need to do." She said I gave her a copy of *The Emotional Side of Job Loss* and said, "My dream is that you'll go home this weekend, read this book, and come back and say, *thanks, now I know what I need to do.*"

She said she went home, read the book, and was especially touched by the quote from Thomas Huxley about doing *what you need to do, when you need to do it, whether you want to or not.* She said she gave the book to her husband, he read it, and then she re-read it on Sunday night and decided she needed to move on and asked me if I would help her to find a new job.

That's why I write, because of that story that I know of. I also have gratitude for all the other people I don't know of, who've read my books and just haven't had the opportunity to say, "Thank you."

I know you are eager to get down to writing your book, but this next exercise is a very powerful one not only while you are doing it, but in the future when you are feeling alone, isolated, overwhelmed, and discouraged.

Exercise #13: Make a list of 50 things you are grateful for. That's right 50. I know that seems like a lot, but really push yourself. I'll even give you 5 to get started.

1. I am grateful for being alive.
2. I am grateful for having a roof over my head.
3. I am grateful for the ability to read and write.
4. I am grateful for my family.

5. I am grateful for the luxury of fretting about writing a book. Other people have far more urgent things to worry about.

6. _____

7. _____

8. _____

9. _____

10. _____

11. _____

12. _____

13. _____

14. _____

15. _____

16. _____

17. _____

18. _____

19. _____

20. _____

21. _____

22. _____

23. _____

24. _____

25. _____

26. _____

27. _____

28. _____

29. _____

30. _____

31. _____

32. _____

33. _____

34. _____

35. _____

36. _____

37. _____
38. _____
39. _____
40. _____
41. _____
42. _____
43. _____
44. _____
45. _____
46. _____
47. _____
48. _____
49. _____
50. _____

Chapter 13
Mentor, Muse, or Publisher?

You're always going to write and draw inspiration from things that you're feeling, things that you've felt. It's kind of impossible not to unless you're writing a song and there's an exact scenario that you're trying to write a song for.

Harry Styles
Singer/Songwriter

Heath and Heath (2010) suggested the best way to get things accomplished is by having someone *dog you*. It's why Alcoholics Anonymous and Weight Watchers are so successful, far more successful than traditional therapy. It's why the most effective way to sustain an exercise program is to have a friend who exercises with you and encourages you to go to the gym, on the days when you both are exhausted. Jakubik (2016) is the leading expert on nurse mentoring. Her research shows that mentor's practice 6 behaviors to help their protégés including: Welcoming, Mapping the Future, Teaching the Job, Supporting the Transition, Providing Protection, Equipping for Leadership. The benefit of those practices is: Feelings of Belonging, Career Optimism, Competence, Professional Growth, Security, and Leadership Readiness. What I am suggesting is a *good* mentor can guide you in your writing journey. It's best if that mentor has expertise in motivation, sustaining momentum, and some of the nuts and bolts of publishing.

I had a great art teacher at Temple University in the 1970's. It was a class in drawing that I took as an elective, but half the class were architect students who were mandated to take the class. Many of them had no artistic talent, stared at the nude model, and drew a stick figure on their paper. The teacher was incredible at finding something good in anything, and providing encouragement. He would look at their stick figure and say, "Wow, I love the way you caught the flow of the model's arm, sweeping through the air. Try and do more sweep motions like that, over and over again." That to me was the how you encourage someone, rather than destroy their ego.

Talking to the *Right* People

One of the other great lessons I learned in life is talking to the right people. Tom Rath (2006) suggested there is no one, perfect friend (or mentor) and we need different friends for the various sectors of our life. I often spoke to the wrong people about going into consulting. I would talk to people I worked with in the Education and Organizational Development Departments about my dream and they'd say, "I tried that once and will never do it again. I nearly went bankrupt. That's why I took this job working in a corporation."

Finally, I met Andy Mozenter, a successful consultant and realized I was approaching this the wrong way. When you benchmark something, you look for people that are doing the best practice, not people who are struggling like you. Andy said, "If you want to go into consulting, I'll help you. You can do it!" He then showed me the steps to take and supported me through the process. So, what I'm suggesting is talk to someone who has published a book or two, not someone who's struggling like you.

Another solution is to use a muse. A muse is defined as a source of inspiration for a creative person. I have several folks in my life who are my *muses*, they laugh at my cartoons, love my stories, and attend my workshops because they say every time they hear me speak, they learn something new. There are lots of people who have turned that sort of relationship into a business of helping people to write book. They will coach you through the process, help with writing skills, and keep you on a timeline to complete your project and get it published. It's not a bad idea, heck maybe I should do a business like that myself?

There is a dynamic in business relationships, that we don't value things unless we pay for them. It's why self-help books don't always work, because it's hard to push yourself to a higher level. It's hard for most people to hold themselves accountable to write, every day, whether they feel like it or not. Yet, for some odd reason, we appreciate things more when we pay a lot of money for them. So, if you feel the need to hire someone to keep you on track, it's not a bad approach. It's why some folks go to a gym for exercise with an instructor, rather than working out alone at home. However, as Heath and Heath suggested, the best coach is still just someone who *dogs* you and you don't need to wonder if they have some ulterior motive and are just doing it for the money.

My Muse

I would be remiss if I didn't share my experience with my main Muse: Dr. Robin Johnson. I have known Johnson for over 40 years. I'm not suggesting you need to know a muse for that long. He provides emotional support, honest feedback, trust, and mutual respect. He is often apologetic in his feedback to avoid hurting my feelings, yet I usually respond by saying, "Hey there's no need to apologize, *good* feedback is a gift and I appreciate it!" My muse keeps me moving by reminding me not to get side-tracked, go off on tangents, or get involved in other projects, but to just keep writing.

The muses feedback needs to be very specific. It can't just be, "I really enjoyed what you wrote. "If the person you're using is a muse is not naturally specific enough you need to ask them probing questions like:
"What exactly did you like?"
"What jumped off the page at you?"
"What do you want to see more of and what should I do a little bit less?"
Here's a very specific piece of feedback I received, "Michael has a real ability to speak in multiple voices depending on the character who is speaking. It's a really important ability that other types of artists and musicians are able to do. It not only brings the character to life, but also sparks the readers interest." It reminds me of the quote from E.L. Doctorow that good writing evokes sensation in the reader that it's not just raining, but what the rain feels like.

My most important piece of advice is: think really long and hard about who you ask for feedback. If you have someone questioning why you're writing, what you're writing about, and suggests it's a waste of time, question what's behind their feedback. Are they trying to help you? Is it helping you? If it's not, run away as fast as you can, because they're your Evil Witch in disguise!

Chapter 14
The Spiritual Side of Writing

I don't believe in 'thinking' old. Although I've transitioned through many bodies - a baby, toddler, child, teen, young adult, mid-life and older adult - my spirit is unchanged. I support my body with exercise, my mind with reading and writing, and my spirit with the knowing that I am part of the Divine source of all life.

**Wayne Dyer
Motivational Psychologist**

Wayne Dyer was a motivational psychologist who wrote one of the best-selling self-help books of all time: *Your Erroneous Zones* (2001). Originally published in 1976, Dyer spoke about guilt, worry, and self-destructive patterns of behaviour that inhibit us from accomplishing things in life. Dyer's practical wisdom offered tips on how to *take charge* of your life, overcome difficulties, and learn to give and receive love. Dyer's father left his mother with 3 young boys and he spent his first 10 years in an orphanage. After graduating from high school, he joined the Navy and afterwards went back to college, obtained a doctorate, worked as a high school guidance counsellor, and then a psychology professor at St. John's University in New York City. He had a traditional academic career, published articles in academic journals, gave lectures, and had a private psychologist practice. His focus was always motivational and at the age of 36 he published his first book documenting his theories. He quit his teaching job and went around the country doing bookstore appearances and interviews "out of the back of his station wagon", according to his publicist. Eventually he went on the lecture circuit, published 20 books, had specials on PBS, and made guest appearances on all the famous talk shows of that era. Dyer's appeal was often attributed to his self-made success, which anyone has the potential to achieve. Dyer's key message was to avoid the guilt other people try to impose on you and take control of your life.

I would be remiss if I didn't talk about my spiritual beliefs about writing. I know it's somewhat of a cliché to say this, but I believe all artists of whatever craft are divinely inspired. Regardless of your spiritual belief or lack of belief, the ideas, inspiration, and connections come from somewhere. Writing is about taking a leap of faith that you are doing something meaningful. You need to find a way to just do it, don't think about it, and pour your heart a soul into it. Only you can determine what it takes to give you that confidence, to be spontaneous, not haunted by your past demons in your head, or worried about what other people think. Many people the find comfort and inspiration through spirituality, a higher power, God, Nature, the Source, or something inside them that cannot be described. Many authors say their source of courage, determination, and persistence comes from their faith. Faith is a very personal thing. Reverend Noble Smith, an Episcopal Minister once told me faith isn't about having proof of something. If you have proof, it's no longer faith. Faith is about believing in something bigger than you, a power you can't necessarily describe, but just believe. That's what trust is all about. It's about taking the leap because you know something stronger than you will take care of the details.

Exercise #14: *Think of a time when you accomplished something you didn't think you were capable of achieving. Did you have a clear goal at the outset? What gave you the inspiration to persist with your efforts to achieve your goal. What did it feel like when you achieved your goal? Can you replicate that process in writing your book?*

Joseph Campbell (2011) suggested atheism is even a belief system, a belief in non-belief. Psychologist Wayne Dyer suggested that Jesus wasn't teaching Christianity. He was teaching the spiritual principles of kindness, love, concern, and peace. He suggested people strive to be Christ-like, or to strive to be like Buddha-like. Dyer suggested that people are often raised to obey the customs, practices, and expectations of organized religions and sometimes miss the foundations spirituality.

Dyer (2011) said he was inspired by the book Three Magic Words (Anderson, 2019). Andersen suggested we have power over things through our thoughts for what you think, is what you will manifest. He suggested that inside us a place of confidence, quietness, and security where all things are known and understood. He suggested the universe knows the answer to all of our "problems" and we needn't struggle, or worry, because when the time comes, the answers will be there. There's a principle called "the great law of attraction," that everything in life that we need for our work and fulfillment will come to us. It is not necessary that we strain about this, only believe! For in the strength of our belief, our faith will make it so. When we take a break (like going on vacation), we see that in the flowers, the trees, the brook, the meadow, and mountains. We realize that something created all these things and that our body is a manifestation of pure spirit, a perfect spirit, that gives us what we need good or bad at any point in time. That's the wonder of it all, if we can remain confident, serene, and sure that no matter what obstacle or undesirable circumstance crosses our path, we refuse to accept it for it is nothing but illusion. There can be no obstacle or undesirable circumstance in you or around you that doesn't serve you in some way. Unfortunately, we don't always see that in the moment. But when we look back, we say, "Oh that's why that happened."

That's how I feel about writing. When you're in the *zone*, it just comes naturally, the words just flow. At other times, it's a struggle, a battle with the voices of doubt in your head. It's at those times where I think about why we struggle in life, the role struggling plays, and either write about that, or set my work aside for another time. As we discussed in previous chapters sometimes sitting things down for a bit is a good strategy, to bring back the magic of writing. Einstein suggested the best research breakthroughs don't always come from long hours of hard work. Sometimes the best inspiration, according to Einstein, came when he took a break, took a shower, and while in the shower, he had an inspirational thought regarding his research.

I leave you with a story (actually one of my cartoons), that I end most of my workshops with, The Starcatcher: *As a young boy walked down the beach at dawn, he noticed an old man ahead of him picking up starfish and flinging them back into the sea. Catching up with the man, he asked him why he was doing this. The old man replied that the stranded starfish would die if left in the morning sun.*
"But, the beach goes on for miles and there are 1,000's of starfish. How can you possibly make a difference?"
The old man looked at the starfish in his hand and then threw it to the safety of the waves. "It doesn't make a difference to this one," he said.

As a young boy walked at dawn the beach an old man ahead of him picking them into the sea. Catching up with the man. The he asked him why he was doing this. The old man replied that the stranded starfish would die if left in the morning sun. "But the beach goes on for miles and there are millions of starfish. How can you possibly make a difference?" The old man looked at the starfish in his hand, then threw it to the safety of the waves. "It makes a difference to this one." he said.

The moral of the story is it doesn't matter to that one person, whether you become a bestselling author, or your book saves the world. It just matters that your book reminded them that they were not alone. That's why you write!

Chapter 15
Final Words

Good writing is supposed to evoke sensation in the reader - not the fact that it is raining, but the feeling of being rained upon.

E. L. Doctorow
Author

Doctorow's book Ragtime was rated one of the 100 best novels of all time. The story took place in the early 1900's and captured the life of fictional rich family in New Rochelle, New York who are friends with a variety of actual famous people during that era. Thus, it loops back and forth between historical fiction and actual facts. The theme of the book is the tension between rich people, the working class, and how to define justice. To me it's the model for an entertaining and thought-provoking book that leaps between non-fiction and fiction.

Here's a quick overview of how to write a book:

1. The secret is not really a secret: Just Write. Just do it!
2. Make yourself an outline of everything you want to include in your book. Just brainstorm ideas, without making judgements. Keep that list and go back to it periodically to stay on track.
3. Don't necessarily write your chapters in order. Write based on the mood you're in today. If you're feeling inspired, write! If you're feeling depressed, lonely, or overwhelmed work on the chapter about those feelings.

4. Look to your past for inspiration. Use every conversation and experience in life as potential writing material

5. Don't question why, just write!

6. Make a list of future projects. Don't question if you should switch to another project, stick to the one you're working on, and add the new idea to your future projects list.

7. Remember we write so others can read to remind them they're not alone

8. Don't fret the details, like cover art, editing, marketing, and distribution. Those things will work themselves out once you have a completed manuscript. For now, just write!

9. Enjoy the journey, have fun with it, don't make it more complicated than it is, you're just writing!

10. If you need a mentor or a muse, feel free to contact me. I'm happy to help.

Exercise 15: Next Steps? *So, what's your plan? What are your next steps? Who can help you in your journey to writing your book?*

References

Andersen, U. S. (2019). *Three Magic Words: The Key to Power, Peace, and Plenty*. San Francisco: Blurb.

Attenborough, R. (Writer). (1993). The Shadowlands [Motion picture]. In B. Eastman (Producer). United States: HBO Studios.

Bass, B. M. (2008). *Handbook of leadership: Theory, research, & managerial applications (4th Ed.)*. New York, N.Y.: The Free Press.

Bachus, N. (2017). *Open Admissions: What Teaching at Community College Taught Me About Learning*. Stockton, NJ: Wild River Books.

Boyle, G. (2017). *Barking to the Choir: The Power of Radical Kinship*. New York: Simon & Schuster.

Bryan, M., & Cameron, J. (1998). *The Artist's Way at Work*. New York: William Morrow.

Cameron, J. (2016). *The artists way: A spiritual path to higher creativity 25th Anniversary Edition*. New York: TarcherPerigee.

Cameron, J. (1998). *The Right to Write An Invitation into the Writing Life*. New York: Jeremy P. Tarcher.

Campbell, J. (2011). *The power of myth*. New York: Random House.

Carnegie, D. (1998). *How to Win Friends and Influence People*. New York: Simon and Schuster.

Csikszentmihalyi, M. (2008). *Flow: The Psychology of Optimal Experience*. New York: Harper Perennial Modern Classics.

Doctorow, E. L. (2007). *Ragtime*. New York: Random House.

Dyer, W. W. (2001). *Your Erroneous Zones: Step-by-Step Advice for Escaping the Trap of Negative Thinking and Taking Control of Your Life.* New York: William Morrow.

Dyer, W. W. (2011). *Excuses Begone!: How to Change Lifelong, Self-Defeating Thinking Habits.* Carlsbad, CA: Hay House.

Grossman, M. B. (2017). *Someone's Got to Do the Work Around Here* Bala Cynwyd, PA: Nurse Leadership Builders available at www.amazon.com.

Grossman, D. (2011). *Did I Ever Tell You About the Time: Leaving a Family Legacy Through Storytelling.* Philadelphia, PA: CreateSpace.

Heath, C., & Heath, D. (2010). *Switch: How to Change Things When Change is Hard.* New York: Crown Business.

Huxley, T. H. (2001). *Collected Essays of Thomas H. Huxley.* Bristol, UK: Thoemmes

Jacobs, A. J. (2018). *Thanks a Thousand: A Gratitude Journey from Bean to Cup.* New York: Simon & Schuster.

Jakubik, L. D., Eliades, A. B., & Weese, M. M. (2016). Part 1: An Overview of Mentoring Practices and Mentoring Benefits. *Pediatric Nursing, 42*(1), 37-38.

Loehr, J., & Schwartz, T. (2004). *The Power of Full Engagement: Managing Energy, Not Time, Is the Key to High Performance and Personal Renewal* New York: Free Press.

Rath, T. (2006). *Vital Friends: The people you can't afford to live without.* New York: Gallup Press.

Shermer, M. (2011). *The Believing Brain: From Ghosts and Gods to Politics and Conspiracies---How We Construct Beliefs and Reinforce Them as Truths.* New York: Times Books

Other Books by Dr. Michael B. Grossman, DM, MSN, RN, NEA-BC, CNML

Someone's Got to Do the Work Around Here: *Overcoming Workaholism*
Do people say you work too much, while you're looking for ways to free up more time for work? Are you stressed when life events get in the way of your work? Is work negatively affecting your physical health? If you answered yes to several of these questions you may want to read more about workaholism, one of the most accepted and encouraged behaviors in our society. If you are looking for more balance in your life, this is the book for you. Rich in experiences, wisdom, time management tips, while still entertaining, and insightful.

Kindness: Figuring out the importance of kindness and its place in the meaning of life is as much an art as it is a crafted science. This is one of those issues that has perplexed mankind since the beginning of time. It is especially challenging to practice kindness when someone is struggling with a marriage, loss of a loved one, or changing their job. Much of the challenge is that everyone has an opinion about what you should do with your life. Whatever the reason you chose to pick up this book, the purpose is to take you on a journey of discovery so that one day you can look back and see your life as an incredible opportunity to be a better person. You have taken the first step by deciding to do something about your life. This book is intended to provide you with a structured approach to increase your level of kindness.

Passion: Finding What Energizes Your Career Do you ever look at a successful person and wonder, "why can't I find a job like that and be successful?" Every one of us is capable of living out our dreams. This book will help you map out your dreams in a step-by-step approach and to successfully achieve your goals to find passion in your work. Passion can be just finding a different way of approaching your current work, so that it is more meaningful, beginning with finding your passion. Successful people love what they do. They wake up in the morning and cannot wait to get to work and jump into the day's activities. You can achieve your dreams too, but in order to achieve them you must map out a plan.

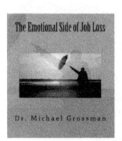

The Emotional Side of Job Loss: It's not how you handle the good times, that matter in life. The true test in life is how you handle tragedy, loss, and the challenge of what to do next. Whether you have lost your job or live with the fear of losing your job, this is the book for you. Job loss can be terrifying and paralyzing. But, there is hope. You can overcome a job loss by realizing you are not alone and applying the steps that other effective people have learned. Yes, if you think it, see it, and believe it you too will be successful again. Read the stories of others who have overcome job loss and follow a step-by-step approach to regaining your confidence, empowering yourself, and find your next career opportunity.

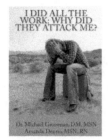

I Did All the Work: Why Did They Attack Me?: Scapegoat Theory in the Workplace The purpose of this book is to identify the dynamics of scapegoat theory, a form of lateral violence. This book is purposefully less than 150 pages. The intention is for you to get an overview of the best body of knowledge about scapegoating, to identify your strengths, and areas you would like to learn more about. You will find a list of references at the end of the book, which will help you on your journey to being more effective in avoiding being scapegoated.

What's Next? Create Your Dream Job With a Plan B is a great way to take a fresh look at your career. The ten chapters unlock the key factors to creating your dream job. This book is direct, yet comprehensive enough to cover all the essential elements to finding a new job or passion in your current work. You can read the book in less than 2 hours and spend as much time as you like working on the exercises to figure out what's next for you.

ALL BOOKS AVAILABLE AT: www.amazon.com

NOTES

CPSIA information can be obtained
at www.ICGtesting.com
Printed in the USA
LVHW110801250420
654346LV00017B/473